LIFT
OFF!

LIFT OFF!

Leadership skills for 7-12 year olds

Paul Canon Harris

Heather Torrens

Illustrations by Jethro Wilson

kevin mayhew

kevin mayhew

First published in Great Britain in 2019 by Kevin Mayhew Ltd
Buxhall, Stowmarket, Suffolk IP14 3BW
Tel: +44 (0) 1449 737978 Fax: +44 (0) 1449 737834
E-mail: info@kevinmayhew.com

www.kevinmayhew.com

9 8 7 6 5 4 3 2 1 0

ISBN 978 1 84867 987 0
Catalogue No. 1501608

Cover and layout design by Rob Mortonson
Cover and book illustrations by Jethro Wilson, www.jethrowilson.com
Typeset by Angela Selfe
Printed and bound in Great Britain

Contents

About the authors

Paul Canon Harris is a writer, speaker and broadcaster. He has wide experience of leadership in a variety of settings. Early experiences of leadership included being Head boy at Royal Grammar School, High Wycombe, class leader at Police Training College and student president at theological college. A qualified teacher and youth worker, he has trained and mentored many young people over a long period. He has been chair of governors of three schools as well as serving on the governing body of a university. Paul is the author of *Leading for a Change* (Kevin Mayhew, 2016). He lives in Bournemouth, with his wife Catherine and their dog, Hope. They have four adult sons and a growing number of grandchildren.

Heather Torrens is a Specialist Leader of Education through the National College for Teaching and Leadership, with many years of experience supporting teaching, learning and music across primary schools in Dorset.

Her leadership experience spans a wide range of teaching and coaching contexts: YMCA youth leadership programmes, developing graduate training students, newly qualified teachers, primary school leaders, and pupils.

Personal research has led to her developing a values-driven spirituality and ethos culture in schools. She is a music and RE specialist whose work has included Motivating Boys, Ethics of Excellence, Real Projects and Super-Learning. In a previous career as a professional musician she performed all over the world and appeared on television. Based in Bournemouth, she is married to Mike and they have two adult children.

Special thanks to **Jethro Wilson** for his inspirational illustrations.

www.jethrowilson.com

Section 1

Section 1

So, you've become a leader!

Congratulations! How do you feel? Excited? Proud? A little nervous? Probably a mix of them all, which is perfectly normal. You have recently become a prefect, a house captain, a head boy or head girl, school council member, a playground buddy or whatever your new title is! Whatever your new role, we hope this brief guide will encourage and equip you for what lies ahead.

Leaders are learners

Leaders come in all shapes and sizes. Lots of different people become leaders. Our personalities and backgrounds shape the way we lead. There are different leadership skills which can be developed. We will give you an opportunity to think about them and discuss them with your friends.

Famous People who were Head girl or Head boy in their school days

- **Joe Hart**, English football goalkeeper for Manchester City and West Ham United.
- **J. K. Rowling**, author of the *Harry Potter* books.
- **Matt Smith**, best known for his role as *The Doctor* in the British television series *Dr Who.*

- **Leigh-Anne Pinnock**, member of *Little Mix* girl pop group.
- **Kate Winslet**, actress.

Factors that make and shape leaders:

- Your home background, characteristics you have inherited and things you have learned by watching others at home.
- Position in family – if you are an older brother or sister, you may be used to leading and caring for others younger than you. If you are a middle

child, you may be skilled in making peace between people, and if you are the youngest, you may be used to being supported or standing up for justice!

- Encouragement from teachers and other pupils.

You may be surprised to have become a leader. Or, perhaps it is something you were hoping for and had worked hard to achieve. Either way, you are a leader because others have chosen you.

Leaders are chosen by others

Over to you:

- **Do you think it takes talent or effort to become a leader?**
- **Think of a leader you admire – they do not have to be famous.**
- **What makes or made them a good leader?**

Section 2

section 2

Reactions – your own and those of other people

Many people will be pleased for you. A few may be jealous or disappointed that they have not been chosen. Not everyone can be a leader, though lots of people can share in leading. Our advice is to enjoy a sense of achievement for a while but do not let it go to your head. No one likes a show-off!

Start as you mean to go on. Like running in a race, you may take a little time to get fully into your stride but the way you start is very important. In this guide you will find tips and suggestions which should help you to be the best leader you can be. Try and do these things from the beginning.

Be humble. People may shower you with congratulations –

do not let it go to your head. Thank people for their encouragement and then try and steer the conversation to other people who have done well, or to another topic.

Deal with any disappointment. In a school setting a new set of pupil leaders are usually chosen at one go. Only one or two can be head boy/girl, house captain, sports leader etc. Some people may feel let down and disappointed. If that is how you feel, choose a safe person with whom to share your feelings, probably a parent. Then decide to do the best you can in your role. Choose to be kind when speaking about, or to, other people. Show you are a good team player. Others will notice this and remember it.

Leaders are humble

What will motivate you:

Some new leaders are happy to lead while it suits them but quickly go off the idea when they must do things they don't like. Try to remember that you are *serving* as a leader. You are going to spend your time and your energy to benefit your fellow pupils and the wider school. People who are leaders at school often go on to be leaders in their adult life. This is an amazing opportunity to learn important lessons which you will use throughout your life.

Ask yourself the Hogwarts Question regularly:

Harry Potter fans will know about Percy Weasley – prefect and head boy at Hogwarts. Percy was *very* ambitious, he wanted to be Minister for Magic.

In *Harry Potter and the Prisoner of Azkaban* Percy Weasley is made head boy. He becomes even more self-important than before. His twin brothers, Fred and George, try to bring him down to earth through their teasing and practical jokes. Avoid being boring or someone people joke about. Try not to take yourself too seriously.

Over to you:

- **How did you feel when you were given a leadership position?**
- **Out of 10, how important is it for you to win? How do you handle losing?**
- **What are you most looking forward to about your new role? Why?**

Section 3

Section 3

Expectations – the things you will be expected to do and be!

Role Model/Example. Younger pupils will look up you. You will be what is known as a *role model*. This means people will watch you when you don't realise it. You will always be an example. Do your best to be a good one!

Ambassador for the school. You may be asked to represent the school at events such as open days and parents' evenings. You may be expected to say a few words to parents.

Communication channel. You may be asked what you think about parts of school life. You can think of ways of improving school life. Perhaps you will have the chance to let the teachers know how other pupils feel, e.g. school council reps.

- **Helping practically with arrangements.** You may be given tasks to do, such as collecting registers, showing new pupils round the school, running a tuck-shop, being a 'buddy' for younger pupils at break time, setting up the hall for assembly, including organising the technology, being a team captain who helps other team members and visitors for sports events.

Leaders serve others

If you have a special badge or a title, be proud of that in a good way. Remember that it means you have responsibility.

Part of growing up and becoming an adult involves going into new situations such as college or a work place. A good way of settling into a new role is to see if you can spot the following things:

- Things you can control
- Things you can influence
- Things you must accept

There is no point using energy and getting worried about things you cannot change. Apply your best efforts to where you can make a difference.

We all like to be appreciated, and you will probably be eager to please. It is good to be motivated in that way. You will find you cannot please everybody. Others' expectations of you are important, but the most important expectations are those you have of yourself.

Set your expectations high but when you miss the mark, as you almost certainly will, be gentle with yourself. Don't beat yourself up, rather learn from your mistakes.

Take some time at the start of your term of office to decide on and set the expectations you will have of yourself. Here are a few examples to get you going. Try and phrase them positively if possible:

- I will try and speak well of other people.
- I will address issues with people face to face, not behind their back.
- I will be an encourager.

Honesty, kindness and forgiveness are values worth holding. If you demonstrate them in your dealings with others, they will repay you very well. We tested the ideas in this book in a school where the pupils chose these values for their school:

Confidence, Compassion, Creativity and Curiosity

Your values are important expressions of your character.

There are many personal qualities associated with leaders. Here are a few.

What would you add?

1. **Direction** – helping a group to decide on a direction.
2. **Inspiration** – leaders use words and examples to inspire others.
3. **Building teams** – good leaders try to build teams. They share leadership.
4. **Acceptance** – leaders are accepted and respected by others. People who force their leadership on others usually become unpopular and unsuccessful.

Over to you:

- **Note down three expectations of yourself in this role.**
- **How important do you think it is to review your successes and challenges?**
- **Decide when you will review it and with whom.**
- **What will people think about you after you have moved on from this school?**

Section 4

Section 4

Self-awareness – knowing your strengths, weaknesses and personal qualities

You may have already thought about why you would be effective in this role. Even if you think you know yourself well, the challenges and opportunities of leadership should help you to become more self-aware. In life, it is through working alongside others, trying new things and facing unexpected situations that we develop and learn more about ourselves.

Leaders need a high degree of self-awareness. This does not come automatically or naturally. Every single one of us has things about us (characteristics and habits) that may sometimes make it difficult for others to work with us. This is why self-awareness is so important. If you are very enthusiastic and like getting on with things, you may not welcome wise advice from a quieter, more cautious person. We need people with contrasting personalities and different skills around us. Team-work is very important.

The book of Proverbs in the Bible is full of ancient wisdom which is useful whatever our background, whether we have any faith or not. One example linked to self-awareness is: 'Wounds from a friend can be trusted' (Proverbs chapter 27, verse 6). In other words, make sure you have one or two friends who give you honest feedback on how you are doing in a positive way. Give them permission to tell you when you need to slow down or to listen more to others.

Getting to know yourself better will also protect you. It will help you deal with criticism and stop you from wearing yourself out by doing too much on your own.

When you are older and as you develop as a leader, you will discover special tests which will help you to understand yourself better. Workplaces sometimes use them when they are recruiting people or as part of their training. Most of them are more scientific than the ones on social media. They are good to do so long as you remember they are never the whole story about you. Do not let them limit you.

Section 5

Section 5

Everybody needs a hero

Who are your heroes? Why do they inspire you?

The word *hero* is sometimes used too much. It used to be applied mostly to people who had been very brave, often those who risked their lives for others. These days it tends to mean people we look up to and admire. We asked a group of 11-year-old pupils the question, 'Who is your hero?' The most popular answers included:

- Taylor Swift
- The Queen
- Mum or Dad
- David Beckham
- David Attenborough
- A favourite teacher
- Usain Bolt
- Bear Grylls
- Stormzy

That's quite a mix of ages and types.

Famous leader

Jesus Christ was an inspiring and surprising leader. He is still admired as a leader, even by people who do not think of themselves as Christians or religious. He turned ideas of leadership upside down. He was different from political and military leaders. Most famously, only hours before being betrayed and arrested he washed his disciples' feet, acting out for them what it means to be a servant leader. He told his followers that if they wanted to lead they must serve others – even if it meant washing their dusty feet!

Here's a story Jesus used when training his friends and followers:

The plank and the speck of sawdust

'Why do you look at the speck of sawdust in your friend's eye and pay no attention to the plank in your own eye? How can you say to your friend, "Let me take the speck out of your eye," when all the time there is a plank in your own eye? You hypocrite, first take the plank out of your own eye, and then you will see clearly to remove the speck from your friend's eye.'

Matthew chapter 7, verses 3-5

Girls versus boys

Sometimes in history, and even in some parts of the modern world, it has been harder for women to be leaders than men. This has been, and is, unfair. Men and women sometimes lead in slightly different ways but there are many examples of great women leaders. Hopefully there will be many more. So, girls – go for it! Do not let anyone (including yourself) hold you back. Be yourself in leadership, bring your own personality and talents to bear and do not let other people's limited views limit you! Young leaders like you and others in your generation will be those who make the breakthroughs that our world needs so much.

When Barack Obama was President of the USA, he and his wife Michelle visited London. Michelle Obama is a successful lawyer, a leader and an inspiring speaker. She chose to spend some time in a local school. She told the girls that she was an example of what is possible when girls from the very beginning of their lives are loved and nurtured by people around them. She said that when growing up she had been surrounded by extraordinary women in her life who taught her about quiet strength and dignity.

Keeping it real: Practical scenarios

1. You are told that another member of your leadership team has been bullying another child in their class. What points do you consider before taking any action?

2. You find out that one of your team has been writing unkind and untrue notes about the deputy head teacher and passing them around. What action do you take?

Section 6

Section 6

Bouncebackability!

That is a strange-sounding word. The clue to its meaning is in the three parts of the word. A football manager was one of the first to use it, probably because he could not think of the word *resilience*. A resilient person is someone who does not become too discouraged or quit when things do not go to plan.

Definition of resilience – *the capacity to recover quickly from difficulties; toughness, the ability of a substance or object to spring back into shape; elasticity.*

Leaders are not quitters

When things go well our confidence gets a boost. When we are criticised we can feel discouraged. Leaders who survive in the long run develop resilience. One way of doing this is to make sure you learn from your mistakes. The successful inventor and business person Sir James Dyson, has said that he expects 'failure' in his exploration and development of new technologies. It took many experimental versions before his Dyson cleaner became one of the bestselling vacuum cleaners in the world.

Michael Jordan was one of the greatest basketball players of all time. It is estimated that he missed more than 9000 shots in his career, lost almost 300 games and on 26 occasions missed a shot that would have won the game. He tells people that he failed repeatedly in his life and that was why he succeeded.

In the world of children's books, the writer Roald Dahl redrafted each of his works seven times before sending them to his publisher.

When others around you make mistakes do not ignore them or think they are useless. The way you deal with others' failures is also an opportunity to encourage and teach them. People are more likely to deal with mistakes in a healthy way if they see their leaders being open and realistic about their own mistakes. Blaming others, making excuses or trying to hide our mistakes are not good responses. Forgiveness and support for others make a school a better place. If people fear making mistakes, they often stop being creative and stop taking risks. There is an old saying, 'The woman or man who never made a mistake, never made anything.'

Section 7

Section 7

Finishing well, moving on, assisting successors

You are probably reading this at the beginning of your year of service, or perhaps even before you begin. You will be surprised at how quickly the time passes. Hopefully this will be because you enjoy serving in this way. You will not have to decide when to stand down; that is fixed by the passing of the year. At some point in your future you may be in paid or voluntary leadership roles and be able to choose when to step back from leadership. Even presidents and prime ministers are governed by constitutions and elections. Leaders can run out of steam. Do all you can to be the best you can, for as long as you can.

Handing on the baton

We have described leadership like running in a race. Decide now to be someone who finishes well. The enthusiasm and thrill of the early months can easily wear off. You will begin to look ahead to the summer and perhaps to starting a new school.

Hopefully, your teachers will help you balance your energy and time. It is a good lesson to learn early. Resist the temptation to take things easy towards the end of the year. Finishing well in a race is even more important than how you start. Look out for signs of a dip in effort or attitude in other members of the team. Encourage each other to keep going.

Relay races are often the most exciting events at school sports days. People hold their breath as the baton is passed from one team member to another. Passing on the baton is important in leadership. If you get the chance, be kind and helpful to your successors.

Toolkit 1

Toolkit 1

Presentation and communication skills

Leaders are often expected to make presentations or to say a few words on special occasions. Many of us get worried about speaking in public. Some people are natural communicators, but most people can improve their communication skills.

Here is some practical advice to bear in mind when making a presentation.

First impressions

- Appearance – look smart, so it is clear you care about what you are about to say or do. If you care, your audience are more likely to. Think – speak slowly and low.

* Understand nerves – when we are nervous we tend to talk hurriedly and quietly. A good tip is to take a deep breath and to look at your audience before you speak.
* Introduction – prepare well and believe in yourself, trust that what you are going to say will be useful, don't try too hard to be funny. Say who you are – unless you think everybody knows.
* Body language – if you can, practise in front of a mirror how you will stand and move. Be aware of what your hands are doing. Avoid covering your mouth, putting hands in pockets, scratching your nose, flicking your hair etc. Think about appropriate gestures. Do not be frightened of a microphone – it is your friend. Imagine it is a favourite ice-cream – stand near enough to be able to lick it (but don't actually lick it!).

Eye contact

* Eye contact is an important part of communication. When we feel anxious, shy or guilty we tend not to look people in the eye.
* For how long should you make eye contact? Between 5-15 seconds with individuals, 4-5 seconds with individuals in a group setting.
* Try to avoid: eye-dart – i.e. rapid glances, this nervous reaction makes others nervous. Slow blink – what it says, another nervous reaction, very off-putting.

Voice

- Relaxation – take one or two deep breaths before starting, look at audience.
- Breathing – steady and controlled.
- Volume and pace – nerves make us gabble and drop our voice. If it sounds slightly slow and loud to you it is probably right.
- Intonation – practise making your voice interesting to listen to, more like a tune going up and down than a one-note song!
- THINK: Relax – Breathe – Project. Music or singing teachers can help you to project your voice. Use your stomach muscles to help project your voice to the back of the room. You should have a sense of your voice coming from deep inside you – though not a tummy rumble!

Structure

- Have brief headings on a small piece of paper to help you.
- Introduction – say what you are going to say.
- Content – say it enthusiastically.
- Summary – tell them what you've told them, briefly.

- Conclusion – the main thing you want people to remember or to do.

Try this . . . Find a partner and take it in turns to say the following sentences:

> *'Regular exercise is good for you. Eating the right food is important too.'*

with: no eye contact, too much eye contact, a boring voice, an excited voice, a low voice, high voice, fast and slowly, confidently and hesitantly.

Toolkit 2

Toolkit 2

Conflict resolution – being peacemakers

Think about this:
If you found yourself needing to resolve a conflict, what would be the things you consider?

When you have spent some time thinking and discussing that question in a group look at the points below. How far do they match your ideas?

Scenario: Lunchtime – you are told that two Year 5 boys are fighting in the playground, watched by a crowd of 20 boys and girls.

- What do you do next?
- What considerations will shape your course of action?

In the heat of the moment:

- Don't run into a fight.

- Assess – Look Listen Speak.
- Start low and slow – do not shout at the top of your voice.
- Take control – probably send someone to get a member of staff.
- Try and separate the two boys if it's safe to do so. Use words before you use actions. If possible, send other people away.

After the event:

- Decide who to involve/not to involve.
- Tell a member of staff what you saw and what you did. Speak calmly and honestly without exaggeration.
- Do not gossip about what happened.
- Think about forgiveness and what will help the boys to make peace.
- Think about how you dealt with the situation and anything you could have done differently. Think about how it made you feel. Talk to someone about any bad feelings you have.

Toolkit

3

Toolkit 3

Leading meetings

Your role as a leader may involve chairing meetings. Depending on your personality, you may not like the idea of having to follow a structure, take notes (often known as minutes) and be organised. In which case, there may be someone else on your team you could delegate the job to. However, it is worth learning this skill for your future adult leadership roles!

- **Be clear on the reason for the meeting**. What is it for? What are your powers? Remember: keep the focus on the main reason for the meeting.

- **What type of meeting is it?** Once only or a recurring meeting? This will probably affect how long it lasts and whether notes need to be taken. Notes are a good reminder of decisions taken and actions proposed.

- **Be clear about who can/should be there.** Make sure you give notice to anyone who should attend so you don't have to use meeting time to send for them! You can ask for support from the adult school leaders for this.

- **Send out notice of meeting and agenda.** This is something adults and good school councils do, so everyone is prepared for the meeting and what will be discussed. It's a great idea to ask people in advance what they want to discuss in the meeting. It will be easier to make decisions. Put these into the meeting's agenda (a list of things to be discussed in order).

- **Book the venue.** Is it available, accessible and appropriate?

- **Arrange in advance for someone to take notes/ minutes.** Do not try and combine this with leading the meeting. Remind any people who are preparing items to be discussed to be ready.

- **Arrive early. Set up the room.** Have spare copies of the agenda available.

- **Keep to time.** Have a clear idea of and state the end time of the meeting, make sure the most important item(s) are dealt with near the start when people are fresh. Be polite but assertive with those who say too much or who repeat themselves. Being assertive means being firm, fair, clear and kind in what you say, even if it is not what another person wants to hear.

End well. Thank people for attending and for their contribution, give the date of the next meeting if known. Beware of spending ages at the end of a meeting trying to fix the next date. Better to propose one or two in advance on the agenda.

To access the free Teacher's Guide, simply go to the home page of our website and key in the book product code (1501608). Then, on the page for *Lift Off!*, click on 'resources' to view or download the pdf.